TETIWE

SHONA

Mhoroyi! Zita rangu ndinonzi TETIWE!

Hello! My name is TETIWE!

NDEBELE

Sawubona! Ibhizo lami ngu TETIWE!

Tetiwe is my grandmother's name. It comes from the Zulu word, **"THETHIWE"** which means One who is trusted.

Language Colour Key

ENGLISH

NDEBELE

SHONA

English: Words connect us. This book shares everyday language in English, Shona, and Ndebele—helping children and families learn, laugh, and grow together.

Ndebele: Amagama asixhumanisa. Le ncwadi yabelana ngamagama ansuku zonke ngesiNgisi, isiShona, lesiNdebele—isiza abantwana lemuli ukufunda, ukuhleka, lokukhula ndawonye.

Shona: Mazwi anotibatanidza. Bhuku iri rinopa mashoko ezuva ne-zuva muChirungu, ChiShona, neSiNdebele—kubatsira vana nemhuri kudzidza, kuseka, nekukura pamwe chete.

TETIWE MY WORDS IN ACTION NDEBELE/SHONA ISBN 978-1-965398-45-6

Compiled & Designed by Alf & Val Clary Muronda
Illustrations by Mehar Afroz
Published By MASAKA PUBLISHING MEDIA HOUSE

MASAKA PUBLISHING
MEDIA HOUSE

TETIWE MY WORDS IN ACTION

Table of Contents

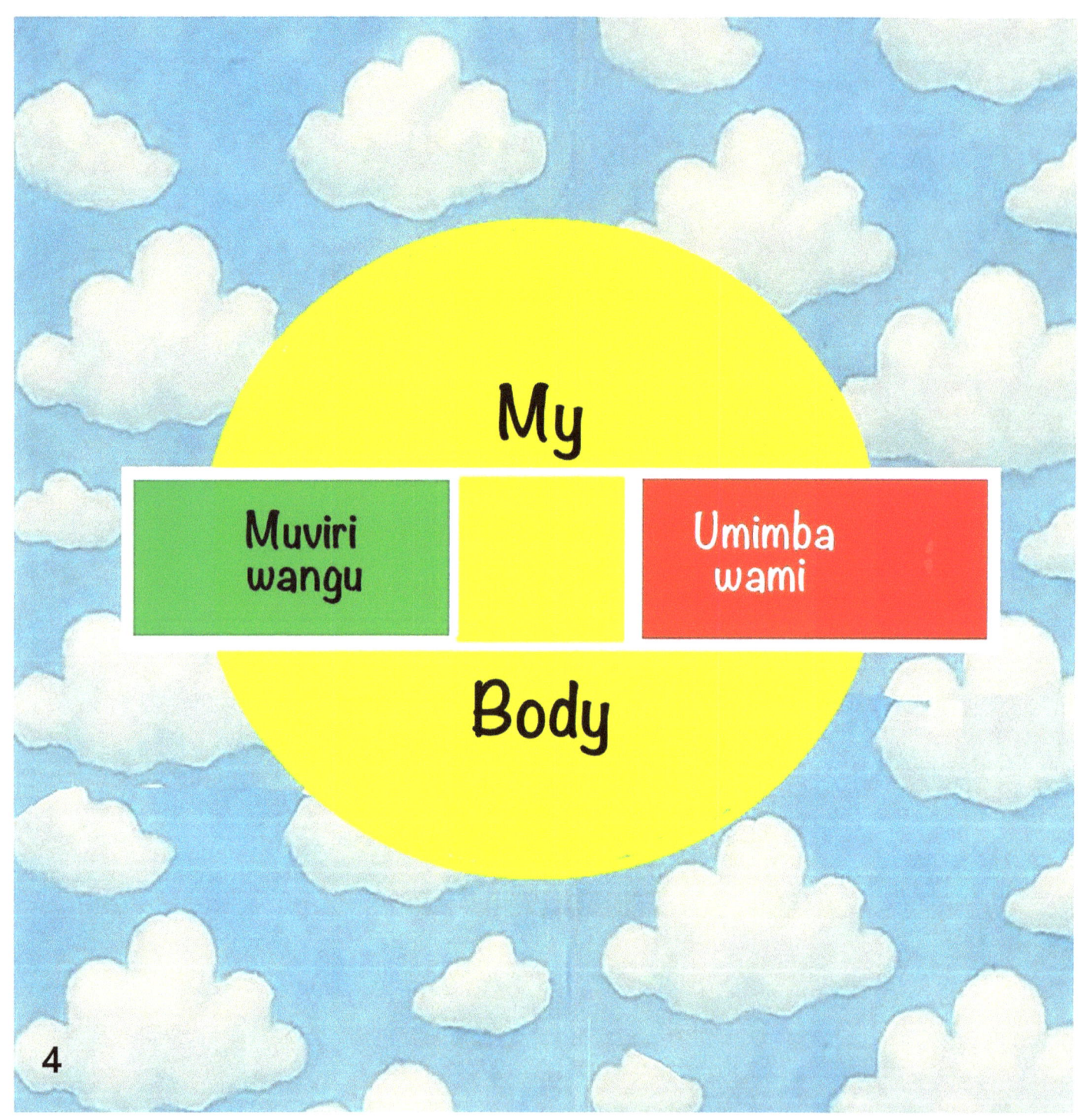

My

Muviri wangu

Umimba wami

Body

4

Parts of
My Body

- My hair
- My eye
- My mouth
- My leg
- My ear
- My hand

Head   Ikhanda   Musoro

Hand   Gumbo

Umlenze

Leg

Isandla   Umlenze

Ruoko

Mouth   Umlomo   Muromo

9

English	Ndebele	Shona
My Hand	Isandla sami	Ruoko rwangu
My Eye	Ilihlo lami	Ziso rangu
Hair	Inwele	Bvudzi
Ear	Indlebe	Nzeve
Nose	Impumulo	Mhuno
Mouth	Umlomo	Muromo
Leg	Umlenze	Gumbo
Teeth	Amazinyo	Mazino
Neck	Intamo	Musoro

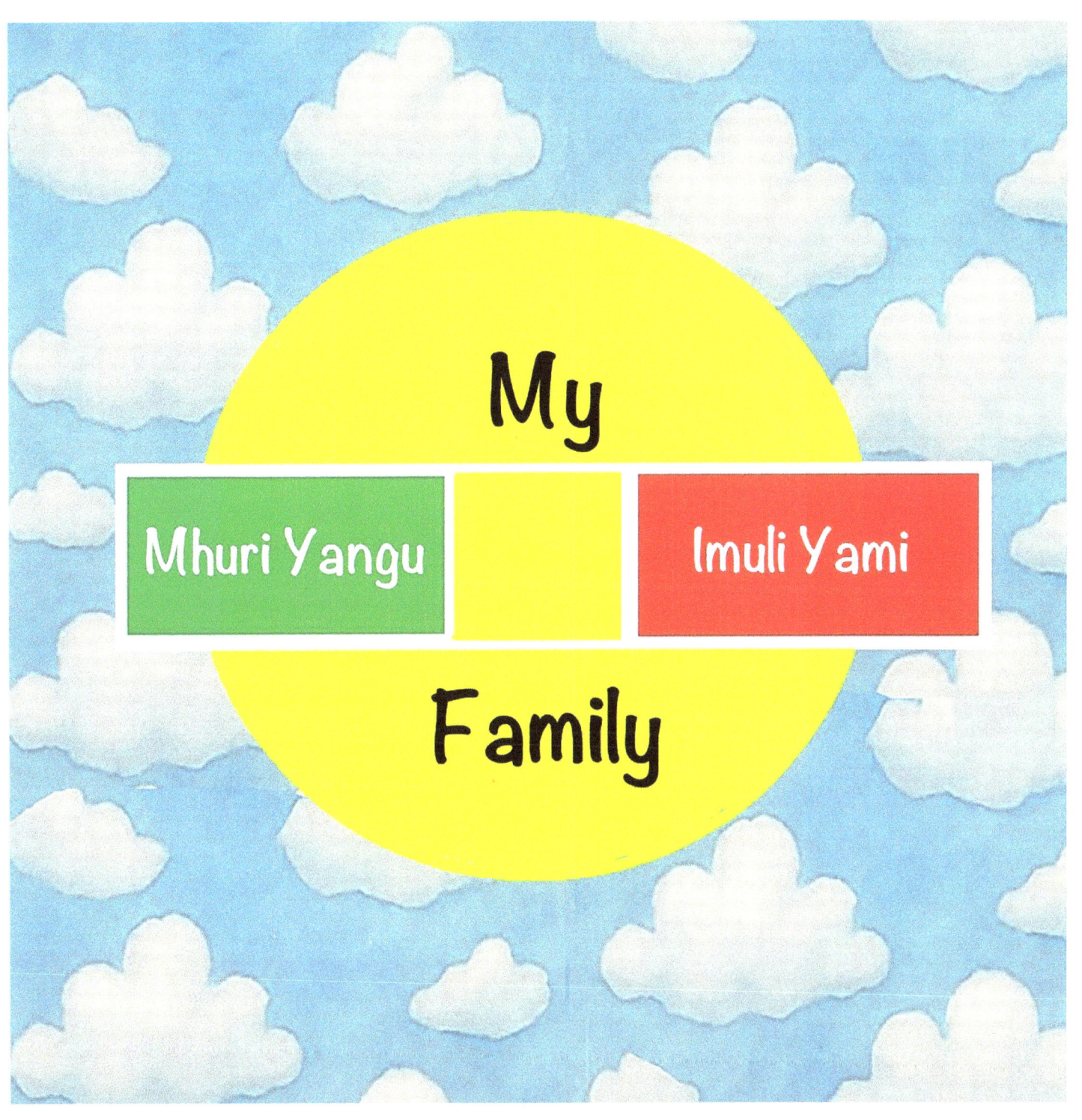

 **Family**

English	Ndebele	Shona
Father	Ubaba	Baba
Mother	Umama	Amai
My Brothers	Abazalwane bami	Hama dzangu
My Grandmother	Ugogo	Ambuya
My Grandfather	Umkhulu	Sekuru

13

14

15

16

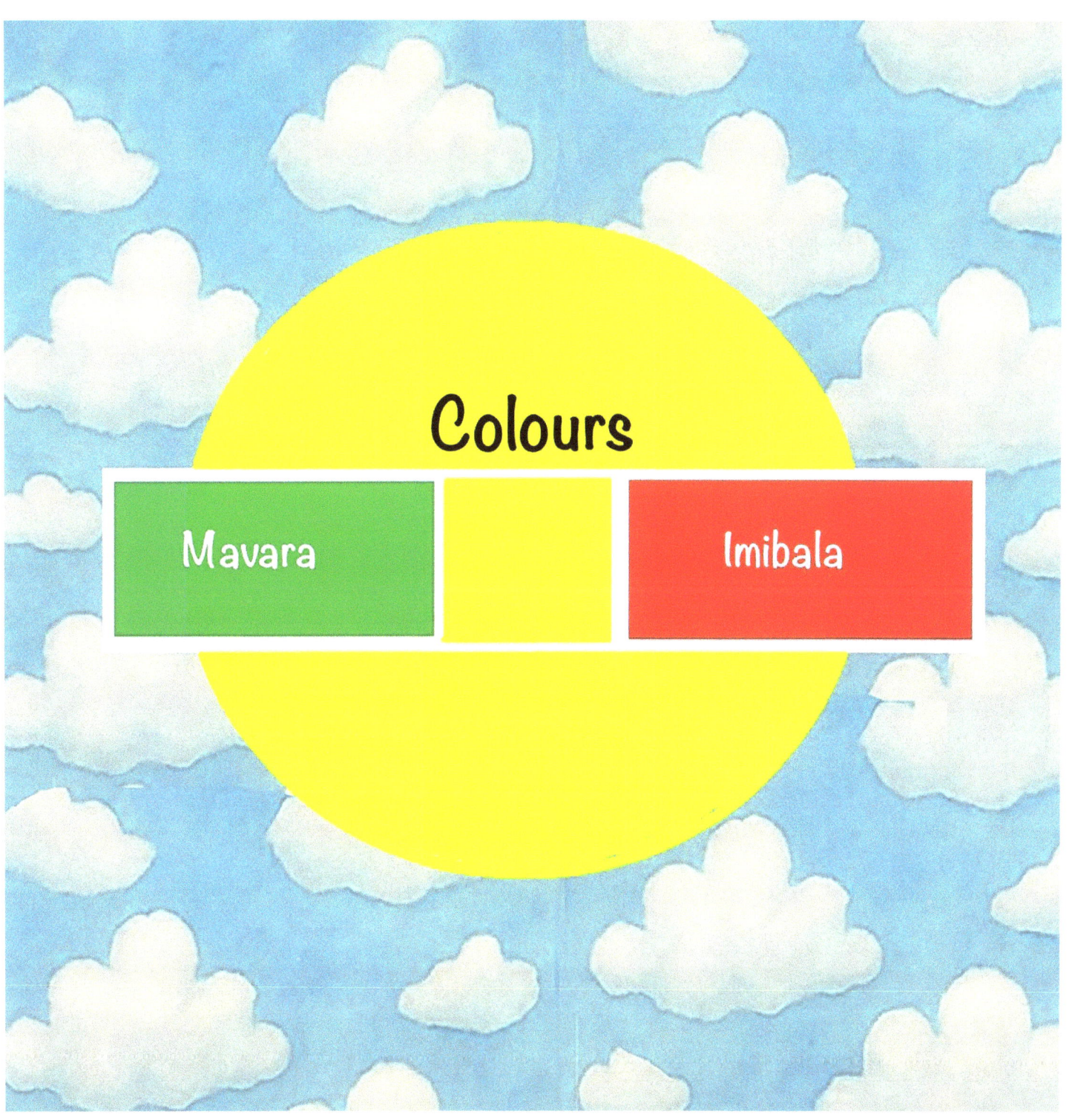

Colours

| Mavara | | Imibala |

🎨 Colours

English	Ndebele	Shona
Colours	Imibala	Mavara
Green	Oluhlaza	Ruhlaza
Red	Obomvu	Tsvuku
Yellow	Ophuzi	Pfumbu
Blue	Oluhlaza okwesibhakabhaka	Bhuruu
Orange	Onsomi	Orenji
Pink	Opinki	Pingi
Purple	Obubende	Pepuru
White	Mhlophe	Chena
Black	Mnyama	Dema
Brown	Nsundu	Ruvanza

My
Colours

Mavara
angu

Lmibala
lami

Green

Oluhlaza

Ruhlaza

Blue

Ruvara rwebhuruu

Okwesibakabhaka

Orange

Onsomi

Orenji

Yellow

Lithanga

Pfumbu

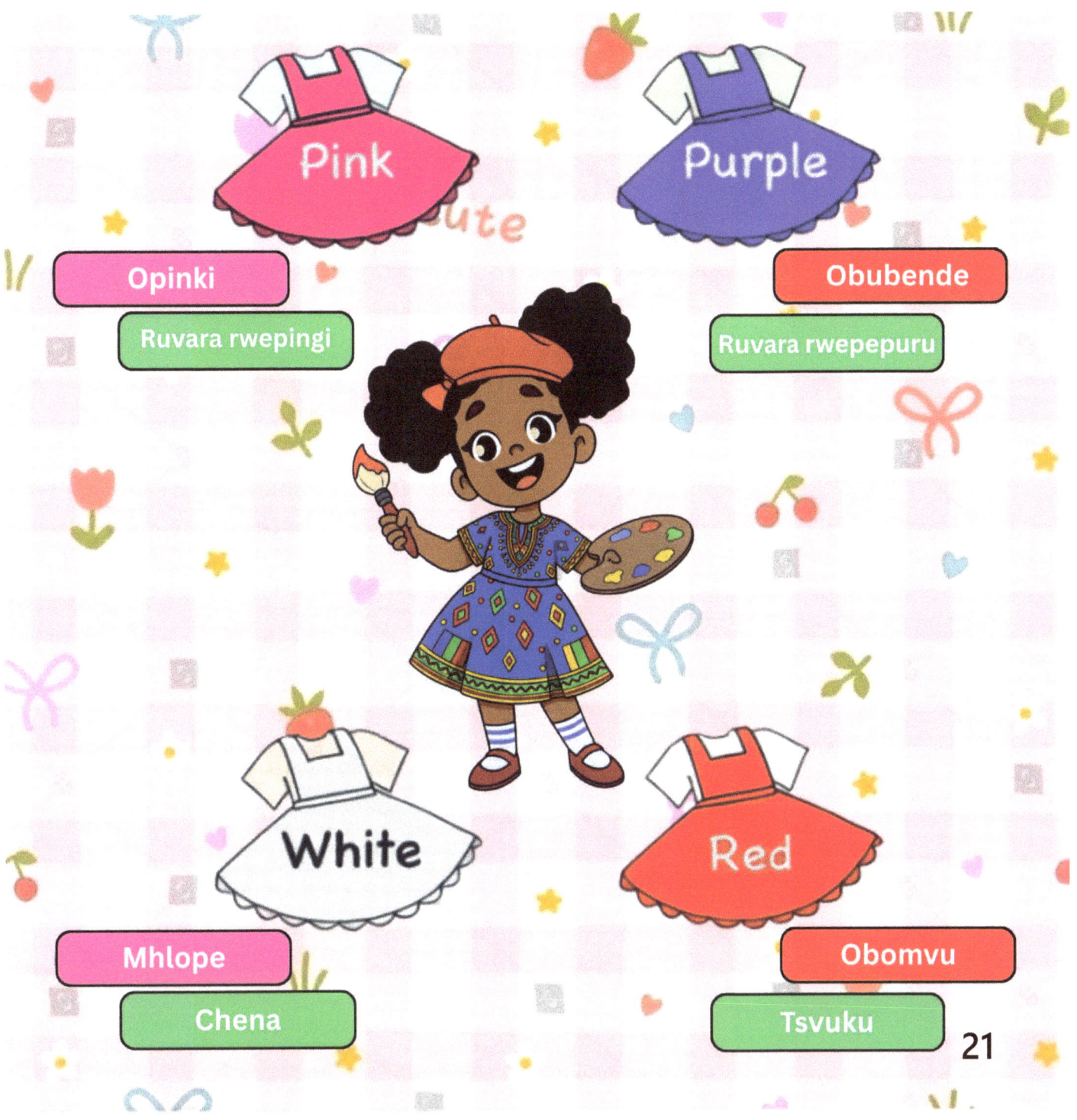

Pink

Opinki

Ruvara rwepingi

Purple

Obubende

Ruvara rwepepuru

White

Mhlope

Chena

Red

Obomvu

Tsvuku

21

Brown

Black

Nsundu

Ruvanza

Mnyama

Nhema

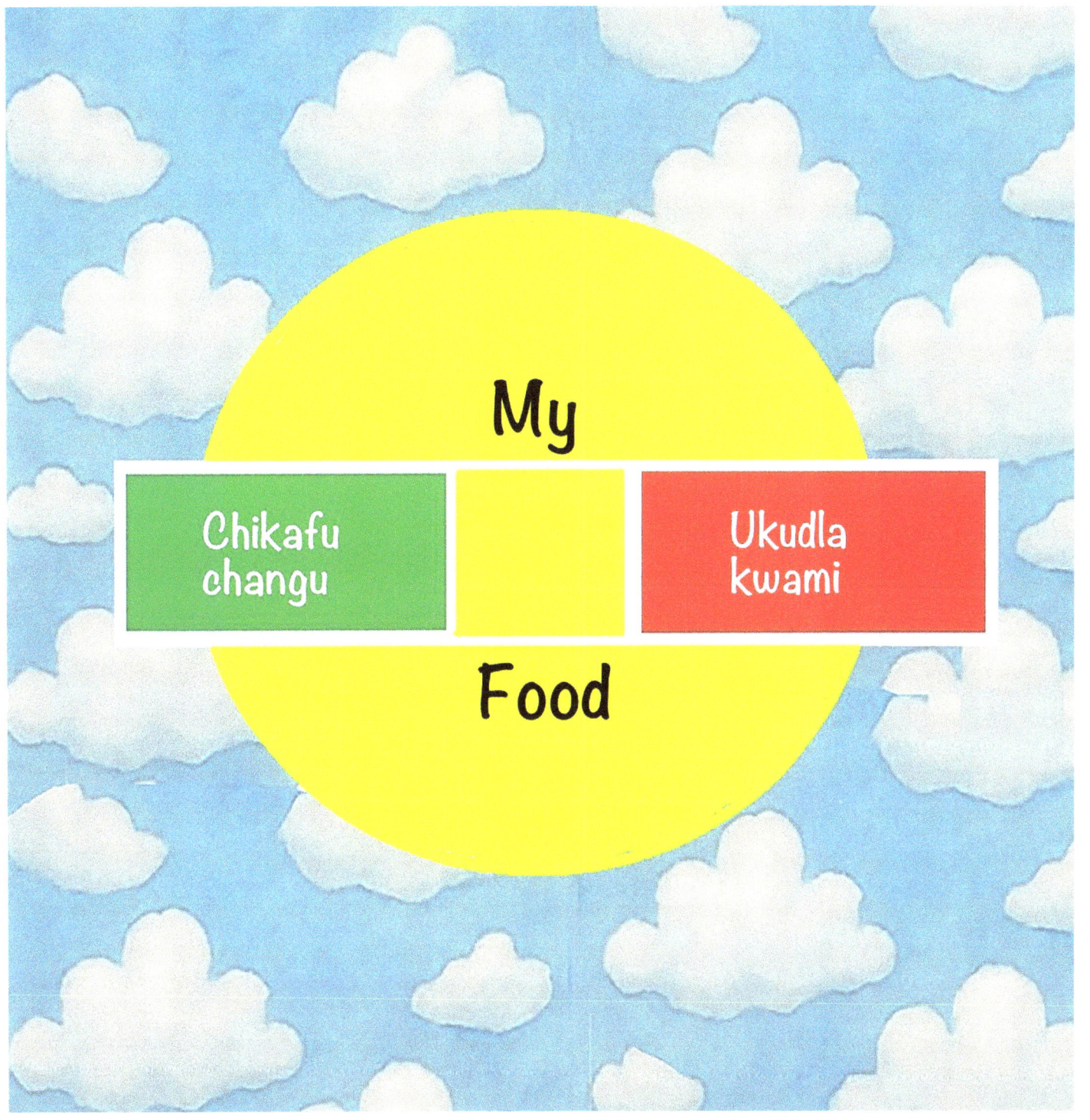

🍴 Food & Drink

English	Ndebele	Shona
Food	Ukudla	Chikafu
Water	Amanzi	Mvura
Milk	Ubisi	Mukaka
Juice	Ijusi	Jusi
Apple	I-apula	Muchero / Apuro
Avocado	I-avokhado	Avhocado
Peanut	Amazambane	Nzungu
Banana	Ibhanana	Bhanana
Ice Cream	I-ayisikhrimu	Ayisikurimu
Bread	Isinkwa	Chingwa
Cake	Ikhekhe	Keke
Chicken	Inkukhu	Huku
Beef	Inyama yenkomo	Nyama yehombe

Apuru

Apple

I-apula

Kotopeya

Avocado

I-avokhado

Nzungu

Peanut

Amazamba

Banana

Banana

I-banana

26

Ice cream
I-ayisikhrimu
Izikirimu

Bread
I-sinkwa
Chingwa

Cake
Ikhekhe
Keke

Chicken
Inkukhu
Huku

Fish
Inhlanzi
Hove

Beef
Inyama yenkomo
Nyama yemombe

28

Maize
Umbona
Chibhage

Porridge
Isitshwala
Bhota

Rice
Mupunga
Irayisi

🍴 Food & Drink

English	Ndebele	Shona
Fish	Inhlanzi	Hove
Maize	Umbona	Chibage
Porridge	Isitshwala	Bota
Rice	Ilayisi	Mupunga
Goat	Imbuzi	Mbudzi
Pig	Ingulube	Nguruve
Cow	Inkomo	Mombe

Animals

Mhuka

Izilwane

Animals that I know.

Izilwane engizaziyo.

Mhuka dzandi noziva.

 Animals

English	Ndebele	Shona
Dog	Inja	Imbwa
Cat	Ikati	Katsi
Donkey	Idonki	Bhasikoro
Lion	Ingonyama	Shumba
Elephant	Indlovu	Nzou
Zebra	Ibhubesi	Mbizi
Hare	Unogwaja	Tsuro
Horse	Ihhashi	Bhiza
Bird	Inyoni	Shiri
Duck	Idada	Bata
Goat	Imbuzi	Mbudzi

Dog
Imbwa
Inja

Cat
Kitsi
Ikati

Donkey
Mbongoro
Idonki

33

Lion
Shumba
Ingonyama

Elephant
Nzou
Indlovu

Zebra
Mbizi
Ibhubesi

Hare
Tsuro
Unogwaja

34

Horse
Bhiza
Ihhashi

Bird
Shiri
Inyoni

Duck
Dadha
Idada

35

Southern Africa

ZAMBIA

ANGOLA

Victoria Falls

Harare

ZIMBABWE

Bulawayo

Etosha NP

Chobe NP

Okavango Delta

Maun

NAMIBIA

Swakopmund
Walvis Bay

Windhoek

BOTSWANA

Kgalagadi Transfontier Park

Gaborone

Kruger NP

MOZAMBIQUE

Pretoria

Maputo

Johannesburg

Mbabane

Fish River Canyon

SWAZILAND

South Atlantic Ocean

Bloemfontein

SOUTH AFRICA

Maseru

Durban

LESOTHO

Indian Ocean

N

36

Cape Town

Port Elizabeth

200 Km

SHONA is spoken primarily in Zimbabwe, with some presence in Mozambique. NDEBELE is spoken primarily in southwestern Zimbabwe and northeastern South Africa.